PUMPKIN CARVING!

A SHOW-HOW GUIDE!

Written by
Renée Kurilla
&
illustrated by
Keith Zoo

ODD DOT • NEW YORK

Hey there!

This **Show-How** gives you the know-how on pumpkin carving. We've included only the essentials so you can easily master the FUN-damentals. With a little practice, you'll soon be carving some goofy and ghostly gourds! Ready? Let's go!

MATERIALS NEEDED:

PUMPKIN

PUMPKIN-CARVING KNIVES
(SMALL, MEDIUM & LARGE)

SPOON

PENCIL

NEWSPAPER OR TABLECLOTH

SPATULA

PETROLEUM JELLY
(OPTIONAL)

LARGE MIXING BOWL

BATTERY-POWERED LED LIGHT OR SMALL CANDLE

TABLE OF CONTENTS

GETTING STARTED

Any size pumpkin will do, though the bigger the pumpkin, the more time it takes to prep. Special pumpkin-carving knives have serrated, or sawlike, edges that makes cutting easier. Extra materials vary per activity. so check the list at the beginning of each chapter. Before you start, follow the steps on the next pages to prep your pumpkin!

TIP: If you are using a candle inside your pumpkin, ask an adult to light it.

HOW TO PREP YOUR PUMPKIN

1

Cover your workspace with newspaper or a tablecloth.

2

Place the pumpkin in the center of your workspace.

3

Draw a big circle on top of the pumpkin to mark the lid.

TIP: A circle works best, but a star shape adds flair!

4

Use a large carving knife to cut along the line.

TIP: Cut the lid at an angle to keep it from falling into the pumpkin!

5

If your pumpkin has a stem, carefully pull up while gently wiggling back and forth to remove the lid. If there is no stem, use a small spatula to remove the lid.

6

Use your fingers or a spoon to scrape any seeds and fibers (the pumpkin guts!) from the lid and place them in a large bowl.

7

Scoop out all the guts from inside the pumpkin and place them in the bowl.

8

When the inside of the pumpkin is totally clean, you're ready to start decorating!

PRESERVING YOUR PUMPKIN

Typically, carved pumpkins last only 3 to 5 days— but you can extend the life of your creation by rubbing petroleum jelly on the cut edges. This will create a seal on the exposed pumpkin and deter animals from eating it!

1

CLASSIC PUMPKIN LANTERN

Let's talk art terms—when you carve a pumpkin, you're working with negative space. Negative space is the space within, between, and around objects. You remove shapes around your image when you carve a pumpkin. A candle inside the carved pumpkin illuminates the negative space to reveal your design!

YOU NEED:

Large Prepped Pumpkin

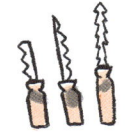

Pumpkin-Carving Knives
(small, medium & large)

Pencil

Newspaper or Tablecloth

Paper
(optional)

**Battery-Powered LED Light
or Small Candle**

1

Cover your workspace with newspaper or a tablecloth,
then place your prepped pumpkin in the center.

2 Use a pencil to draw eyes, a nose, and a mouth on your pumpkin.
Here are a few different examples of features you can draw:
TIP: If you need extra practice, sketch the face on paper first!

EYES	NOSES	MOUTHS

3

Use a small carving knife to carefully cut out your shapes. Take your time!

4

As you finish each shape, pop it out of the pumpkin with your fingers from inside and remove it from your workspace.

TIP: Throw away these pieces, make compost, or use them for the pumpkin puree recipe on page 46.

5

Remove any remaining pumpkin guts and smooth out the carved edges with your fingertips.

6

Place a battery-powered LED light or candle in the middle of the pumpkin, making sure it is level.

TIP: Use a serving spoon to level the bottom if necessary.

7

Replace the lid, turn out the lights, and enjoy your new, glowing pumpkin friend!

If you cut a star-shaped lid, rotate it so that it sits on top of (instead of within) the pumpkin. It will let out some extra light!

2

GOOFY GOURDS

YOU NEED:

Large or Medium
Prepped Pumpkin

Tiny Pumpkin
(to fit inside your larger
pumpkin)

2 Oblong Gourds

Pumpkin-Carving
Knives
(small, medium & large)

Candy Corn

Newspaper or
Tablecloth

Pencil

Toothpicks

Battery-Powered
LED Light or
Small Candle

Black Permanent
Marker

1

Cover your workspace with
newspaper or a tablecloth,
then place your larger,
prepped pumpkin
in the center.

2

Use a pencil to draw exaggerated eyes, a nose, and a mouth on your pumpkin. Here is an example, but don't be afraid to get creative!

3

Use a small carving knife to cut out your shapes. Take your time!

4

As you finish each shape, pop it out of the pumpkin with your fingers.

5

Remove any remaining pumpkin guts and smooth out the carved areas with your fingertips.

6

Push toothpicks through the bottom of a few pieces of candy corn.

7

Stick the other end of the toothpicks into the pumpkin's mouth to make candy-corn teeth.

8

On the sides of your carved pumpkin, trace the small ends of your gourds and carve holes along your trace lines.

9

Push the small ends of the gourds inside the holes to make goofy arms!

10

Use a permanent marker to draw a silly or spooky face on your tiny pumpkin. Above are a few examples.

TIP: Carve a face into your tiny pumpkin if you like, but don't forget to prep it first!

11

Lower the tiny pumpkin inside the larger pumpkin, near the mouth.

12

Place a battery-powered LED light or candle behind the tiny pumpkin.

13

Replace the lid, turn out the lights, and enjoy your new, glowing pumpkin creation!

There are so many creative ways you can carve and design! Place your gourd arms and tiny pumpkin in different places for silly effects. Sometimes people pose the pumpkin guts like, well, you know . . . it makes me sick!

3

PUMPKIN HOUSE

YOU NEED:

Tiny Pumpkin or Gourd

Large or Medium Prepped Pumpkin

Pencil

Pumpkin-Carving Knives
(small, medium & large)

Black Permanent Marker

3—4 Small Leaves

Toothpicks

Craft Moss

4—5 Acorns

Newspaper or Tablecloth

3—4 Pinecones

2—3 Medium or Small Rocks

Hot Glue and Hot Glue Gun

2—3 Flowers

Battery-Powered LED Light or Small Candle

1

Cover your workspace with newspaper or a tablecloth, then place your prepped pumpkin in the center.

2

Use a pencil to draw a door on your pumpkin. Here are a few examples, but feel free to get creative:

3

Draw some windows on your pumpkin, even around the back! Here are a few examples:

TIP: Remember that you'll be carving out the negative space, so give yourself enough room to maneuver.

4 Use a small carving knife to cut out your door and windows.

TIP: If you accidentally cut out a smaller piece like a windowpane, reattach it with a toothpick.

5 As you finish carving each shape, pop it out of the pumpkin with your fingers.

Don't throw away or lose the door piece!

6 Remove any lingering pumpkin guts and smooth out the carved areas with your fingertips.

7

Draw and carve out a small window in the center of the door piece.

8

Make a hinge by sticking a toothpick in the top left side of your door.

9

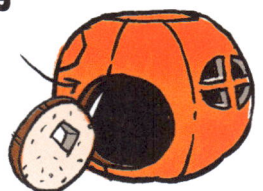

Carefully insert the door with toothpick into the door frame to make an entry that opens and closes.

10

Decorate the outside of your pumpkin with moss, acorns, rocks, and leaves. Apply hot glue to the back of each object and hold in place on the pumpkin to let it set.

11

Draw a silly or spooky face on your tiny pumpkin or gourd.

Here are a few examples:

12

Lower the tiny pumpkin or gourd inside the larger pumpkin house near the door.

13

Place a battery-powered LED light or candle behind the tiny pumpkin or gourd.

14

Replace the lid, turn out the lights, and enjoy your new, glowing pumpkin house!

Stack smaller carved pumpkins on top to make a pumpkin high-rise! Use battery-powered LED lights inside so it doesn't get too hot.

4

PRECISION-SCULPTED PUMPKIN

YOU NEED:

Large or Medium Prepped Pumpkin

Curved U-Tip Carving Tool

X-Acto Knife

Pencil

Printer Paper

Masking Tape

Toothpicks

Newspaper or Tablecloth

Battery-Powered LED Light or Small Candle

1

Cover your workspace with newspaper or a tablecloth, then place your prepped pumpkin in the center.

2

Draw a design on a sheet of printer paper. Fill the whole page!

Feel free to get creative!

3

Tape your design to the pumpkin.

4

Use a toothpick to punch holes along the lines of your design into the pumpkin.

5

Remove the paper from the pumpkin.

TIP: For easier carving, punch enough holes so that your design is visible on your pumpkin.

6

Use an X-Acto knife to chip away at the pumpkin's shell—but don't go all the way through! You should see lighter-colored pumpkin flesh as you carve.

7

Use the curved U-tip carving tool to continue sculpting until you complete your entire design.

8

Place a battery-powered LED light or candle in the middle of the pumpkin.

9

Replace the lid, turn out the lights, and enjoy your new, glowing pumpkin!

You can etch words into your pumpkins, too!

BOO!

5

SPOOKY DIORAMA

YOU NEED:

Large Pumpkin *(unprepped)*

2–3 Tiny Pumpkins or Gourds

Spoon

Large Pumpkin-Carving Knife

Spatula

Pencil

Craft Moss

7–8 Medium or Small Sticks

Black Marker

Black Construction Paper

Acorns, Rocks, and Small Leaves (3–4 each)

Toothpicks or Skewers

2–3 Tissues

Small Pinecones and Flowers (2–3 each)

Newspaper or Tablecloth

5" (13 cm) String

Hot Glue and Hot Glue Gun

Scissors

Battery-Powered LED Light

Tape

1

Cover your workspace with
newspaper or a tablecloth,
then place your large
pumpkin in the center.

2

Use a pencil to draw a large circle
on the front of the pumpkin.

3

Carve out the circle with a large
carving knife, then use a spatula
to remove it.

4

Scoop out all the guts from
inside the pumpkin.

5

Smooth out the carved edges
with your fingertips.

6

Place some craft moss in the bottom
of your carved pumpkin for grass.

7

Hot-glue some sticks together to make trees. The size of your pumpkin will determine the size of your trees.

8

Poke your tree sticks into the bottom of the pumpkin.

9

Use a pencil to draw 3 bats on the black construction paper using the steps below.

10

Cut out the bats and tape toothpicks to one side of each bat.

11

Stick the bats into the top inside of the carved pumpkin at different heights.

TIP: If you want to alter the bats' heights, use skewers instead of toothpicks!

12

Layer your tissues on top of each other, then pick them up together from the middle.

13

Tie the string around the tissues about 1" (2.5 cm) from the top, leaving a long tail.

14

Draw a spooky ghost face with marker on the tissue.

15

Tie the end of the ghost's long string to a toothpick.

16

Stick the ghost's toothpick into the top of the pumpkin, making sure that the length of the string fits well in your diorama.

17

Design and arrange your tiny pumpkins or gourds inside the pumpkin.

18

Place a battery-powered LED light inside the pumpkin, behind the objects.

19

Arrange the rest of your objects inside the pumpkin.

20

Turn out the lights and enjoy your pumpkin diorama!

Instead of a single light, try fairy lights or a spooky strobe light!

6

PAINTED CAT PUMPKIN

YOU NEED:

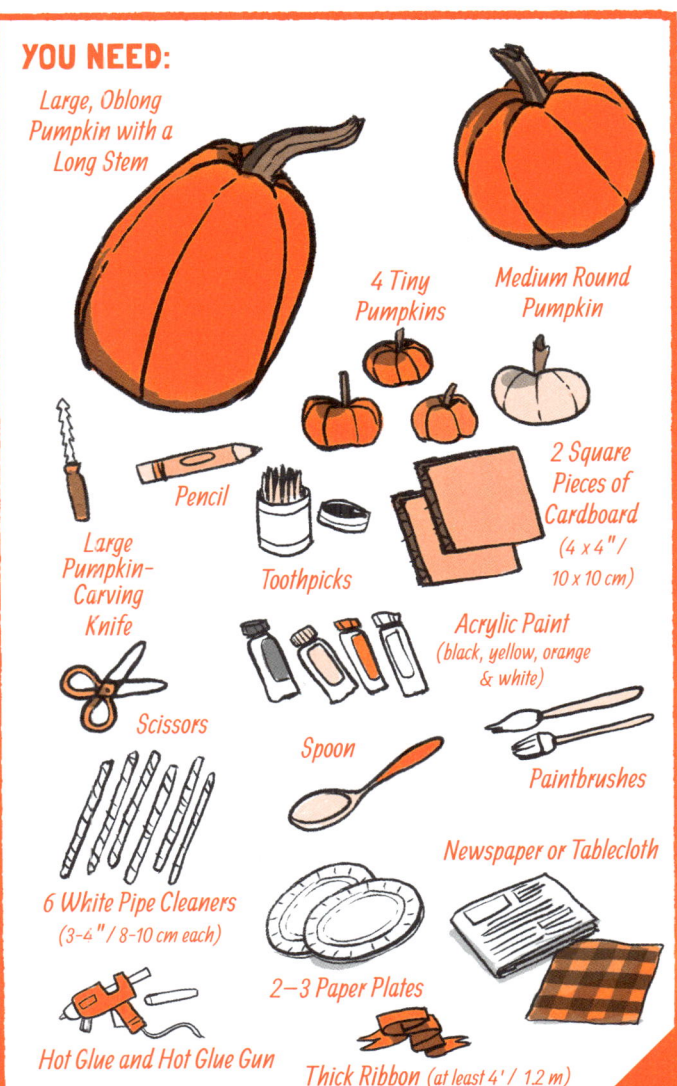

Large, Oblong Pumpkin with a Long Stem

4 Tiny Pumpkins

Medium Round Pumpkin

Large Pumpkin-Carving Knife

Pencil

Toothpicks

2 Square Pieces of Cardboard (4 x 4" / 10 x 10 cm)

Acrylic Paint (black, yellow, orange & white)

Scissors

Spoon

Paintbrushes

6 White Pipe Cleaners (3-4" / 8-10 cm each)

Newspaper or Tablecloth

2-3 Paper Plates

Hot Glue and Hot Glue Gun

Thick Ribbon (at least 4' / 1.2 m)

1

Cover your workspace with newspaper or a tablecloth.

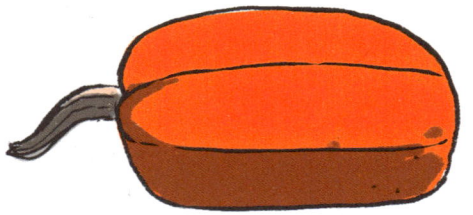

Place the large, oblong pumpkin sideways in the center of your workspace. Use the flattest side for the bottom.

2

Draw a carving line around the stemless end of the oblong pumpkin that's big enough to set the medium pumpkin inside.

3

Use a large carving knife to cut out the shape.

4

Remove the carved shape and scoop out the pumpkin guts.

5

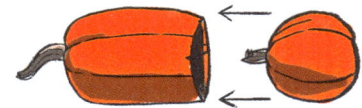

To make the cat's head, place the medium pumpkin slightly inside the larger pumpkin, stem-first.

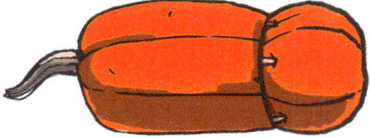

TIP: Secure the head with some toothpicks. Don't worry if it doesn't match up perfectly!

6

Pour some black paint on a paper plate.

7

Paint all of your pumpkins black, then let them dry.

8

While the paint is drying, cut two triangle shapes out of the cardboard. These will be the pumpkin cat's ears!

9

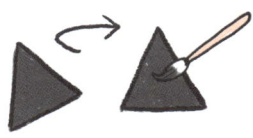

Paint the cardboard triangles black on both sides, then let them dry.

10

Wrap the ribbon around the pumpkin cat's neck to make a collar,
then use hot glue to secure it in place.

11

Pour some yellow, orange, black, and
white acrylic paint on a paper plate.

12

Add the cat's eyes with
yellow paint.

13

Add the cat's fur with
white paint.

14

Add the cat's nose and mouth
with orange and black paint.

15

Use hot glue to attach 3 pipe-cleaner whiskers to each side of the nose.

16

Use hot glue to attach the cardboard ears to the top of the head.

17

Place the tiny pumpkins at the base of the body to create the illusion of little feet. Now you have a pumpkin cat!

Since all pumpkins are different shapes and sizes, you can make some really fun (and funny-looking) creatures!

7

FESTIVE FEEDERS

This is a two-day project!

YOU NEED:

Large or Medium Pumpkin

Pumpkin-Carving Knives
(small & large)

3 Pieces of Rope
(6' / 2 m long and ¼" / 6 mm thick)

Spatula

Spoon

Baking Sheet

Strainer

1

Carve off the top of your pumpkin.

2

Scoop out and wash the pumpkin seeds in a strainer.

3

Spread the seeds in a flat layer on a baking sheet and let them sit overnight to dry.

4

Carve 3 small holes around the top of the pumpkin's opening.

5

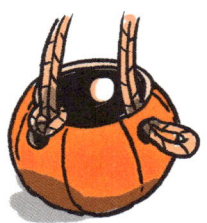

Fold each rope in half, then feed each loop through the holes. Secure the loops with lark's head knots.

6

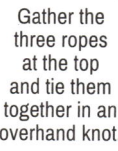

Gather the three ropes at the top and tie them together in an overhand knot.

TIP: Check out *Show-How Guides: Knots* for more ways to tie interesting, useful knots!

7

Use a spatula to place the dried seeds inside the pumpkin.

8

Hang the pumpkin outside and wait for visitors!

KEEP IT SIMPLE: BOWL FEEDER!

1

If you don't have rope, simply carve off the top of your pumpkin and use it like a bowl instead!

2

Carve four holes around the top, then feed two long sticks through the sides for birds to perch on!

If the pumpkin seeds get eaten quickly, refill the pumpkin with store-bought birdseed.

BIRD SEED

FLOWERPOT PUMPKIN

YOU NEED:

Large or Medium Prepped Pumpkin

Scissors

Nonserrated Kitchen Knife

Floral Foam or a Jar with Water

Medium Bouquet of Wild or Store-Bought Flowers

Newspaper or Tablecloth

1

Cover your workspace with newspaper or a tablecloth, then place your prepped pumpkin in the center.

2

Hold the floral foam under running water until it has absorbed as much as it can.

TIP: If you use a jar of water, make sure your pumpkin's interior has a flat bottom so the jar doesn't tip over.

3

Place the wet foam inside the pumpkin. If it sticks out the top, slice the foam with a nonserrated kitchen knife.

4

Separate the filler stems in your bouquet from the flower stems. (Filler stems are usually the bushier greens in a bouquet.)

5

Cut at least 1" (2.5 cm) from the bottom of each stem.

6

Push the filler stems into the floral foam to cover as much area as you can.

7

Arrange the flower stems! If any stem seems too long, cut it shorter to make it fit. Keep going until you run out of stems.

TIP: Make sure all of the stems go at least 2" (5 cm) into the foam so they can absorb the water.

8

Freshen your flowers every day by adding a little water to the foam (or, if you are using a jar, lift it out to refill it).

Display your flowerpot pumpkin near a window, but out of direct sunlight!

PUMPKIN PUREE

Pumpkin puree is the main ingredient in pumpkin pie—make it yourself using any size pumpkin piece you've carved!

1 Preheat oven to 400° F (200° C).

2 Lay parchment paper on a baking sheet.

3 Put your carved pumpkin pieces on the parchment paper with the skin side up. If you are using a whole pumpkin, cut it in half, remove the stem, and place each half on the parchment paper, skin side up.

4 Roast until you can easily poke a fork through and pull it out (about 30–40 minutes, depending on the thickness).

5 Take the baking sheet out of the oven and let cool for an hour.

6 Scoop the pumpkin flesh away from the skin and into a bowl, then discard the skin.

7 Use a food processor to blend the pumpkin until it is smooth. Add water as necessary for the right consistency.

8 Keep your puree in the refrigerator for up to a week!

Add pumpkin puree to pancakes, muffins, oatmeal, cookies, yogurt, pasta, and more for a nutritional boost—and a yummy pumpkin flavor!

ROASTED PUMPKIN SEEDS

1 Preheat oven to 300° F (150° C).

2 Wash the seeds thoroughly, removing any extra bits, and strain.

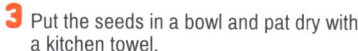

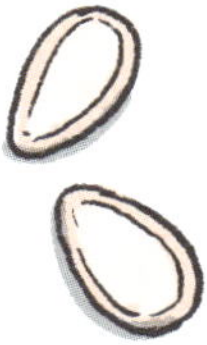

3 Put the seeds in a bowl and pat dry with a kitchen towel.

4 Stir in about 2 tablespoons (30 ml) of melted butter. Use more or less based on the amount of seeds you have.

5 Spread the seeds in a single layer on a baking sheet.

6 Sprinkle the seeds with salt to taste. Add any other seasonings you may like!

7 Bake for 45 minutes or until golden brown, stirring them every 10 minutes with a spatula.

ENJOY!

I like adding cinnamon!

An imprint of Macmillan Publishing Group, LLC
120 Broadway, New York, NY 10271 • OddDot.com

ISBN 978-1-250-78435-3
Library of Congress Control Number 2021046304

Editor: Kate Avino
Designer: Christina Quintero

Our books may be purchased in bulk for promotional, educational, or
business use. Please contact your local bookseller or the Macmillan
Corporate and Premium Sales Department at (800) 221-7945 ext. 5442
or by email at MacmillanSpecialMarkets@macmillan.com.

Show-How Guides is a trademark of Odd Dot.
Printed in China by Hung Hing Off-set Printing Co. Ltd., Heshan City,
Guangdong Province
First edition, 2022

10 9 8 7 6 5 4 3 2 1

Keith Zoo and Renée Kurilla

are a husband-and-wife artist/author team living in Massachusetts. See more of their work online at keithzoo.com and kurillastration.com, and on Instagram and Twitter @keithzoo and @reneekurilla.